Molly
the mallard duck

The true story of Kathy and the mallard duck she named Molly

Written by Karen J Tapp
Illustrated by Karen A Welch

Order this book online at www.trafford.com
or email orders@trafford.com

Most Trafford titles are also available at major online book retailers.

 www.trafford.com

North America & international
toll-free: 844 688 6899 (USA & Canada)
fax: 812 355 4082

Our mission is to efficiently provide the world's finest, most comprehensive book publishing service, enabling every author to experience success. To find out how to publish your book, your way, and have it available worldwide, visit us online at www.trafford.com

Because of the dynamic nature of the Internet, any web addresses or links contained in this book may have changed since publication and may no longer be valid. The views expressed in this work are solely those of the author and do not necessarily reflect the views of the publisher, and the publisher hereby disclaims any responsibility for them.

ISBN: 978-1-4669-8524-7 (sc)
978-1-4669-8523-0 (e)

Library of Congress Control Number: 2013905773

Print information available on the last page.

Trafford rev. 02/17/2022

We hope you enjoy this story and it makes you laugh.

Karen J Tapp

Kathy A McGinnis

Karen A Welch

Every spring, ducks everywhere make nests,
lay their eggs, and tend to the nest until their offspring hatch.
This may have happened in your backyard.
It is nature at its best. This usually happens,
often unnoticed, and rather uneventful.

But not when the duck chose the front yard of my sister.
Kathy took it upon herself to see to the
safety and well-being of the duck she
named Molly and her ducklings
once they hatched.
And so this story began one spring day...

I would like to dedicate this book to my sister,
Kathy McGinnis
It is her whimsical style and unique personality
that brought this story to life.
I would like to thank Karen Welch
for adding her artistic illustrations
to make this story come alive.

Once upon a time,
there was a lady named Kathy
who lived with her husband, Gordon,
in a community in Strongsville, Ohio.
They lived in a large home with a
light post in the front yard.
Around the light post were bushes.

One day,
Kathy was weeding
around the bushes.
To her surprise, the bushes
started to move!

2

She peeked into the bushes and found

a mallard duck sitting on a nest of eggs.

3

Kathy named the duck Molly. Now being a loving and nurturing person, Kathy worried about the well-being of Molly. She brought out a bowl of water and bread and pushed it close to her nest.

She thought about putting up a fence to keep the other animals away.

4

She checked on
Molly
every morning
and every night.

By the third day,
she noticed that Molly
had not eaten any food
or drank any of the water.
"You have to eat to stay
strong," she whispered
to Molly.

5

Kathy went in and called the people who protect wild life for advice.

They told her that mother nature takes care of wild life and Kathy should not worry. They told her that a duck will sit on her eggs until they hatch, only leaving briefly at night. Once hatched, she will immediately leave the nest and head for the pond to join her mate and the other ducks. They told her the fence was not a good idea. While other animals could not get in, Molly could not get out.

One warm spring night, around one in the morning,
with the window open, Kathy heard a terrible noise.
A cat screeching, a duck quacking,
something was terribly wrong.

QUACK   QUACK

OH NO!!!

The ducklings
had hatched.

Kathy looked out of
the window in time to
see a cat running away.

Molly was chasing the cat.
The ducklings were following.
Molly was in trouble!

8

Kathy ran outside to see
if she could help.

9

Molly chased away the cat.
She worried about
the safety of her
newly hatched ducklings
that were following
close behind her.

She decided to go back to the nest
to keep her ducklings warm
from the cool night air.

10

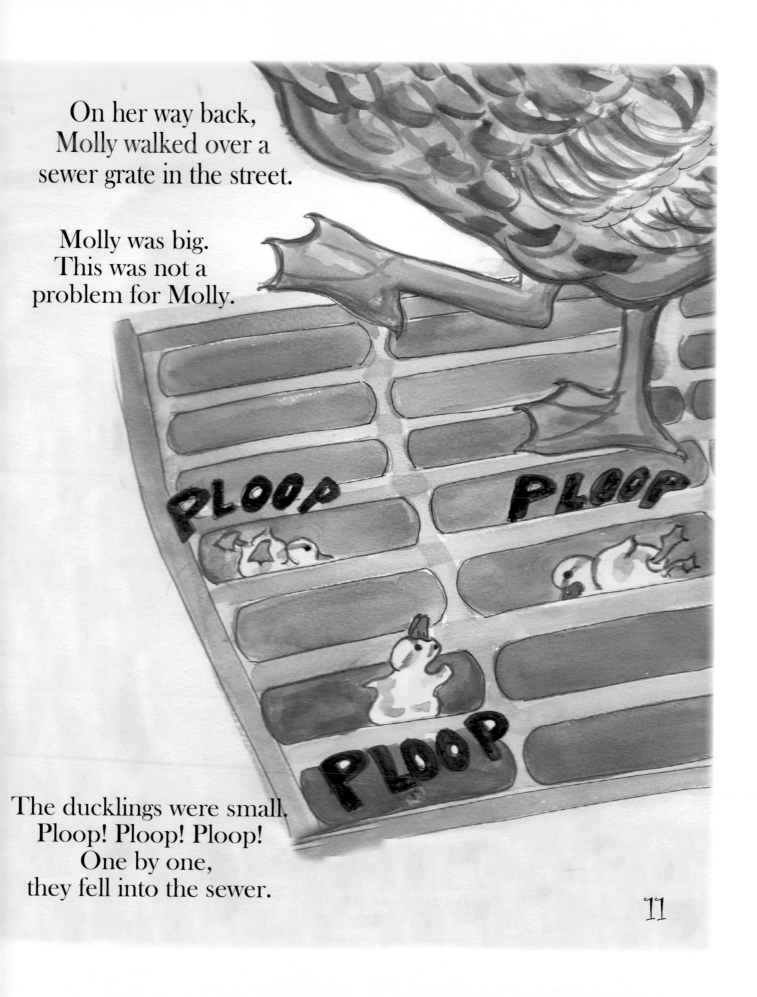

On her way back,
Molly walked over a
sewer grate in the street.

Molly was big.
This was not a
problem for Molly.

PLOOP PLOOP

PLOOP

The ducklings were small.
Ploop! Ploop! Ploop!
One by one,
they fell into the sewer.

Molly was pacing by the sewer
quacking and squawking
and making a terrible noise.

Kathy thought the whole neighborhood
would wake up with all that noise.
No other lights went on.

Kathy went back in the house to get a flashlight.
She looked down in the sewer to see the situation.
There was water in the sewer and
they were swimming in the water.

There was another pipe that connected to the sewer
that went under the street. As long as
the ducklings remained in the sewer, they were safe.
If they swam in the pipe that ran under
the street, who knows where they would go.
It was too far down for Kathy to reach.   13

What to do, What to do???

I know,
thought Kathy.
I'll call the police,
or maybe
the firemen.
Or both!

She didn't know if
either would come, but
she made the call anyway.
It must have been a slow
night in Strongsville.
They dispatched
a fire truck and
3 police cars.

14

Upon arriving to the scene, the policemen and firemen
were quite amused with Kathy
and her genuine concern for the ducklings.

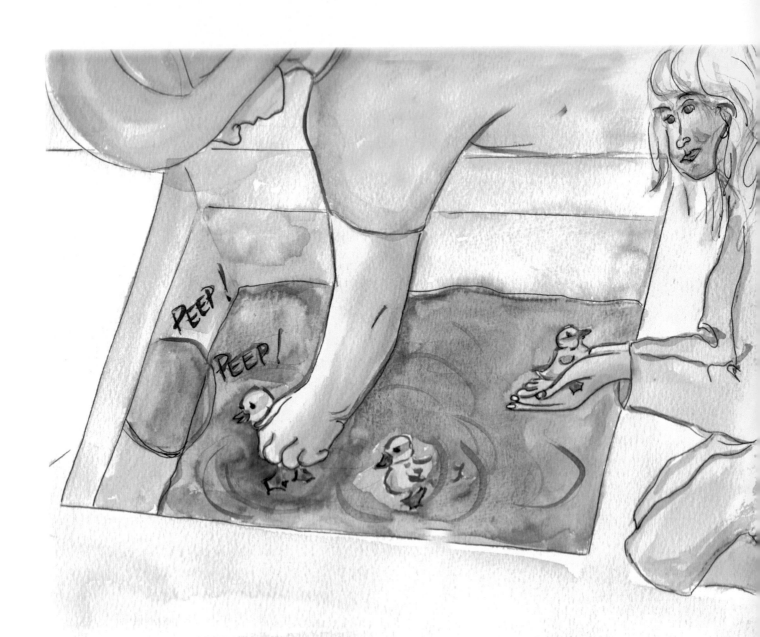

One of the firemen was a large man with long arms.
He removed the sewer grate, and he laid down on the ground.
Reaching down, he snapped up one of the ducklings,
then another. He handed them to Kathy. She put them
down near the frantic Molly, who was
pacing and quacking the whole time.

He put his arm down again, but no third duckling.
They needed more light than the flashlight provided.
The police cruisers turned their cars
so the headlights all pointed at the sewer.

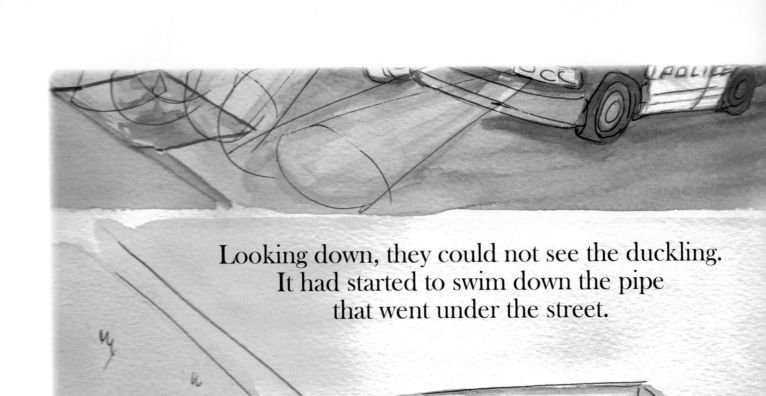

Looking down, they could not see the duckling.
It had started to swim down the pipe
that went under the street.

There was a ledge to step down into the sewer.
One of the policemen, a smaller man, stepped forward
to go down into the sewer.

If the duckling had not swam too far,
maybe he could reach it.

18

A few minutes later, the policeman
came up from the sewer
with the duckling safe in hand.

He handed the duckling to Kathy,
and she turned to hand it to Molly.

Molly was nowhere to be found.

The firemen and policemen bid farewell to Kathy
and went back to work.

Kathy took the duckling and walked
thru her neighbors' yards looking for Molly.

"Molly, Molly," she called.
Molly was nowhere to be found.
Molly took her two ducklings and left.

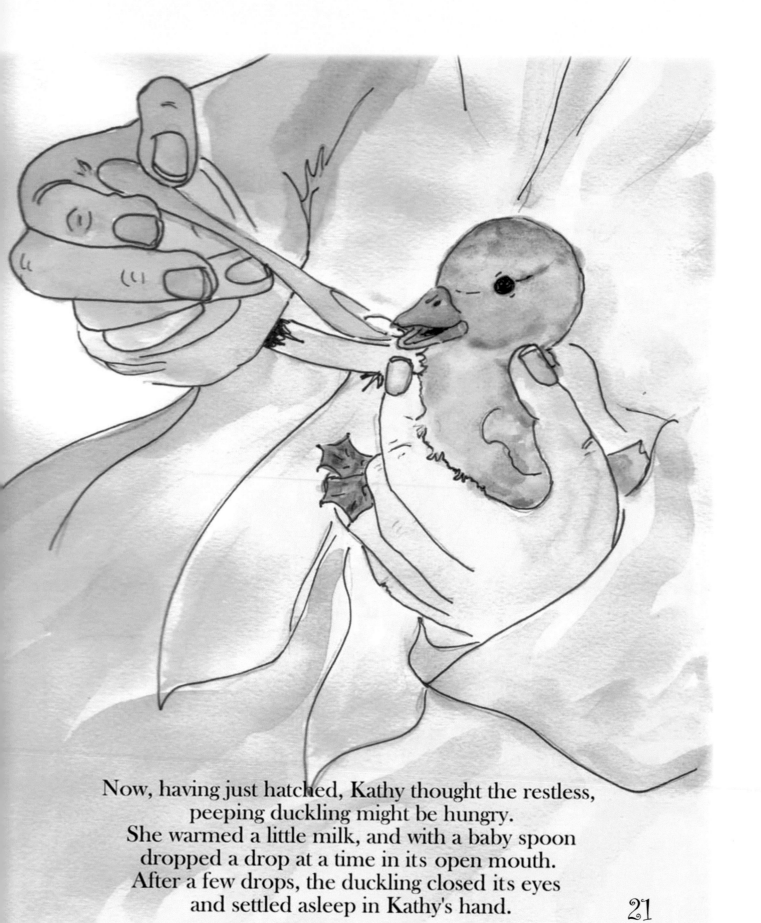

Now, having just hatched, Kathy thought the restless,
peeping duckling might be hungry.
She warmed a little milk, and with a baby spoon
dropped a drop at a time in its open mouth.
After a few drops, the duckling closed its eyes
and settled asleep in Kathy's hand.

21

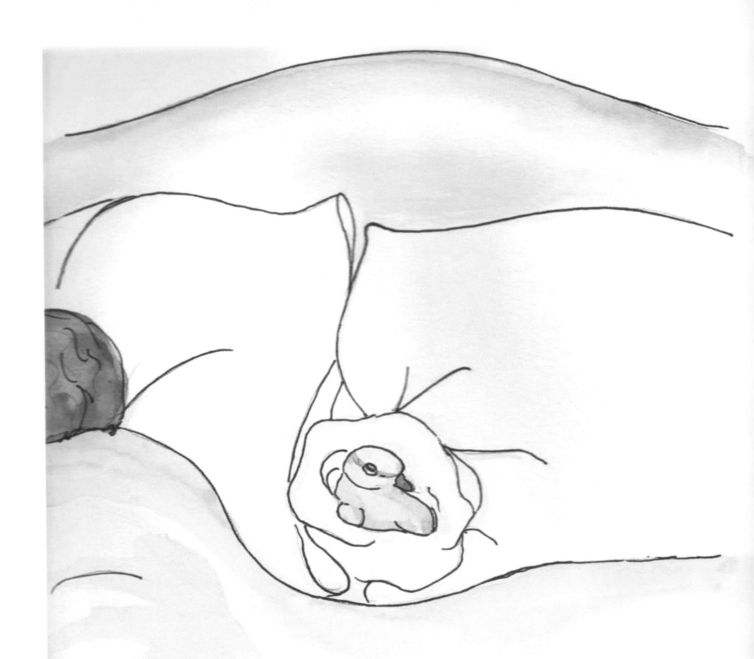

Kathy wrapped the duckling in a towel
and tucked it between the pillows in her bed.
Tomorrow, she would take the duckling
to the lake to look for Molly.
For now, they both needed some sleep.

It was somewhere around 5 a.m. when the
little duckling's hungry tummy woke it up.
It started peeping and wiggling and woke Gordon up.
"That sounds like a duck! Why does it sound so close?"
"Don't roll over, Gordon, or you will squish it," said Kathy.
She told him of her adventures of the night as he laughed.

"Well, you know you can't keep the duckling."
"I know" replied Kathy as she got up
to take the duckling to the
lake to find Molly.

Once at the lake, with the
duckling in hand, she wondered.
How would she ever find Molly?
There must have been a dozen
other mallards with their new families.
"Molly, Molly," she called.
"I have your baby."

Kathy set the little duckling down.
It started peeping.
One of the mallard ducks
started flying towards them.
Kathy stepped back as Molly
came forward to claim her duckling.

25

When Kathy put the duckling down
she noticed a mallard duck flying
towards her in full aerial attack,

as if to say, "give me my baby back."
Kathy noticed Molly's panic
and ran for safety.

26

A year later, in the spring, Kathy noticed two mallards in the yard. They appeared to be looking for a place to build a nest.

Kathy thought, "could it be Molly?"
Why yes, it was...
The End!

27

Printed in the United States
by Baker & Taylor Publisher Services